THE MALA
of
GOD

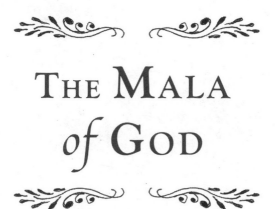

THE MALA
of GOD

MOOJI

NON-DUALITY PRESS
An Imprint of New Harbinger Publications

Dedicated to

My Master
Sri HWL Poonja
Papaji
the Divine Lion
whose grace swallowed me

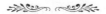

and to my mother
Euphemia Hamilton
who in life was a Lion of Christ

WAY IN

he Mala of God is more than a book. It is a celebration of the living God, a blessing made tangible to be absorbed inside the Heart. The power of true prayer is to be in direct communion with the One. It is to discover, experience and imbibe the Truth of the unchanging God, to rise above our lowliness and mere fleshly nature, to be confirmed in the joy of unity with the One beyond the concept of unity and oneness, to be completely merged in the Supreme.

We intuitively experience God as the core of our innermost being. God is life itself and more than this. He is the totality of all that is, ever was and ever will be—what is potential, what is revealed, what is realised beyond separation. All is the Awareness God-Self.

To some, it may sound like a contradiction that one who has realised the Truth, the God-Self, would utter any such thing as a prayer, or speak of God as his Father when he is the very essence himself. But it is not a contradiction; the prayer of an awakened being is a true prayer, for it never leaves the One. It is out of his very Oneness, out of the love and joy that emanates from the awakened heart, that these prayers come as a gift to this world.

The Mala of God is offered to all seekers and devotees of Truth. For the devotee must develop wisdom and discernment, just as the philosopher must develop trust, openness, love and surrender to the Divine. One who has realised the Truth finds no conflict in its myriad expressions but sees the same presence of the One in all.

When the sage prays, draw near to him, for it is pure sentient expression bowing to its Source. Be absorbed in his Oneness. He will introduce you to God directly, for his presence radiates divinity and is the very embodiment of Truth. When the heart-mind encounters this presence, it is instantly struck and becomes naturally baptised in the Unborn Awareness Self.

Drink from his chalice of love and wisdom stirred by the finger of God. Even one prayer fully swallowed is enough to set your heart free in the infinity of Being. Be so drunk that you will find your way home without a map. Enter this temple of emptiness.

LISTEN

LET NO MAN SAY
WHAT GOD IS
OR WHAT GOD IS NOT

RATHER
LET HIM KEEP QUIET
INSIDE HIS BEING
UNTIL HE FINDS HIS
LORD HERE

Who can separate from
the All-Encompassing One?

In Him
just be
completely drowned
completely immersed
saturated
emptied
burnt
crucified
and beautified
by His holy presence

just say Yes
inside your heart
and be empty
be exchanged
for Him

Let this life be
for nothing else

108 Prayers

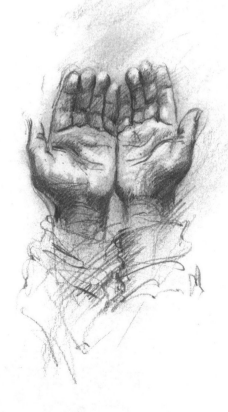

Beloved

Be thou my Friend

FATHER
LET THIS DAY
NOT BE A DAY SPENT IN THE MIND
BUT A DAY ABSORBED IN UNITY WITH YOU
INSIDE THE HEART FOR
ALL ETERNITY

OM

BELOVED FATHER
WITHOUT YOU I AM NOT
I AM—THUS I KNOW YOU ARE
THIS KNOWLEDGE THIS KNOWING
IS THE SWEETEST THING

HOW AMAZING IS YOUR PLAYFULNESS
HOW SUBTLE ARE YOUR CLUES

O BELOVED
YOU HAVE TAUGHT ME NOT TO FEAR
THINGS OF THE MIND OR THE WORLD
BUT TO TURN MY FACE
AND FIX MY EYES
UPON YOU
ALONE

NOW
ACCORDING TO THY WORD
ABSORB MY MIND COMPLETELY
IN THEE

O Light of Life
let me cease being me
rid me of this burden urgently

Let me exist by the light
of your eyes only

DIVINE LION OF BEING
LET ME END UP IN YOUR INESCAPABLE JAWS
BECAUSE ONE BITE FROM YOU
WILL PRODUCE NO SCREAMING
BUT ONLY PERFECT SILENCE
NOW AND FOREVER

LET ME REMAIN ETERNALLY
IN THE BELLY OF GOD

HALLELUJAH

AMEN

O Perfect One
Remove the sense of
I and other
Remove all desires
conscious and unconscious
Make healthy body and mind
for Thy service alone

Let me be ever established in You
Ungraspable One

DIVINE FATHER
YOU ALONE PERMIT ME
TO COMMUNE WITH YOU DIRECTLY
FROM THE HEART OF THE I AM

WHO ELSE BUT YOU COULD RAISE
A MERE PERSON INTO
THE STATE OF HOLY PRESENCE

HALLELUJAH!

BELOVED FATHER
YOU STRIKE ME
SO AS TO INSTIL HUMILITY
INSIDE MY BEING

PLEASE KEEP MY HEAD
ALWAYS AT YOUR FEET
UNTIL I MERGE WITH YOU
HERE

O GRACIOUS SELF
I CAN DO NOTHING BY MYSELF
YOU ALONE ARE LIFE AND EXISTENCE
AND THE ONE APPEARING TO LIVE THEM

YOU ARE THE ONE SELF IN ALL

HALLELUJAHOVAH
JAH RASTAFARI

BELOVED FATHER
ERASE THE MEMORY OF ME
CLOSE MY ACCOUNT
OF PERSONAL IDENTITY
AND ITS SEEMING TREASURES

RID ME OF EGO
AND ABSORB ME IN YOU
O UNBORN AWARENESS

MY LOVE
MY HEART WAS TWO FULL
SO 'I' HAD TO LEAVE
NOW WITH YOU
THE ONE
ALONE HERE
ALL PAIN IS GONE
AND PERFECT JOY REMAINS

SUCH SWEET DEPARTURE

O
LORD OF HEARTS
THANK YOU
FOR ALLOWING ME
TO BE
NOTHING

BELOVED
I AM
IS ONLY YOU

HOLY MOTHER
YOU ARE THE SOLE GURU
THE WOMB OF ALL MANIFESTATION
WISDOM AND LOVE
ARE YOUR FRAGRANCE

WHO ELSE IS THERE TO MENTION
BASICALLY

FATHER
YOU GIVE ME PLEASURES
SO I CAN LOOK AWAY FROM YOU
YOU SEND ME FEAR
SO I CAN SEEK REFUGE
IN YOU

GIVE ME EYES TO SEE
NOTHING APART FROM YOU

BLESSED FATHER
LEAVE NOTHING HERE
THAT IS CAPABLE OF MAKING A CHOICE

OF WHAT USE IS DISCERNMENT
WHEN THERE IS ONLY YOU?

BELOVED
EVEN TO LOOK INTO
THE MIRROR OF SELF-INQUIRY
IS IMPOSSIBLE WITHOUT
YOUR GRACE

O UNFATHOMABLE LORD SIVA
YOU WHO ARE PURE AND
TIMELESS AWARENESS ITSELF
DISPEL NOW
ANY REMAINING DELUSION HERE

SRI ARUNACHALA SIVA
OM

HOLY SPIRIT
LIKE REVERSING A GLOVE
YOU TURNED ME INSIDE OUT
THUS EXPOSING
THERE WAS NOTHING HERE
IN THE FIRST PLACE

WELL...
NOTHING BUT YOU

O
HEART OF HEARTS
YOU HAVE STOLEN MY MIND AND PERSON
AND REPLACED THEM WITH
YOUR HOLY PRESENCE

WHO DESERVES
SUCH GOOD FORTUNE

O
ONE AND ONLY
YOU ARE
OUR SOLE REFUGE
LIGHT OF OUR HEART
THE SOURCE OF TRUE LOVE
OUR SELF SUPREME

BENEVOLENT FATHER
NO ONE CAN FIND
THE TRUTH WITHOUT YOUR GRACE
NEITHER DETERMINATION
NOR TECHNIQUE ALONE
CAN REACH YOU
O GAPLESS ONE

FRUSTRATED ARE THE ARROGANT
WHO FAIL TO SEE YOUR TIMELESS
AND OMNIPRESENT FACE
EVERYWHERE

WHERE IS THERE A PLACE
FOR ANY WITHOUT YOU

BELOVED FATHER
MY HEART IS BURSTING
ONLY TO SAY THANK YOU
THANK YOU
THANK YOU

BUT I WONDER
IF A ME IS NEEDED
TO FEEL THIS SWEET GRATITUDE
NEED THERE BE A SEPARATION?

IN MY HEART
THERE IS NO DUALITY
ONLY THIS UNFADING ESSENCE
INEFFABLE

YOU ALONE ARE HERE

IF THIS IS NOT SO
IF THIS IS NOT TRUE
THEN LET THIS MOMENT BE ONLY
TO PUT AN END
TO THE ILLUSION
OF ME

BELOVED
NOW IT IS SEEN THAT
THIS PAINFUL FEELING
OF SEPARATION FROM YOU
ONLY PERSISTED DUE TO
MY PERCEIVING YOU
AS 'YOU'
AND NOT
AS I

WHAT IS THERE TO ACCEPT OR REJECT
WHEN YOU HAVE STILLED
MY MIND AND HEART
IN THE HOLLOW OF YOUR BEING

JAH LIVE!

O TIMELESS ONE
FROM THE GRAVE OF PERSONHOOD
I HEARD YOUR VOICE AND
FELT YOUR LIFE-GIVING KISS
INSIDE MY BEING
YOU BROUGHT ME BACK TO LIFE
BY BREATHING THE BREATH OF
JNANA AND BHAKTI
INTO MY SOUL

LET ME NEVER AGAIN FALL ASLEEP
IN YOUR OMNIPRESENCE

ONCE TOUCHED BY
YOUR SWEET PRESENCE
I COLLAPSED AT YOUR HOLY FEET
AND BEGAN FALLING UPWARDS
INTO THE LIGHT OF YOUR INFINITE FACE

THIS LIGHT PERVADES MY ENTIRE BEING
AND SHINES AS UNFADING
LOVE PEACE AND JOY

ALLAHLUIA

SUPREME FATHER
WHICH DIRECTION MUST I LOOK
TO FIND YOU WHO ARE
TIMELESSLY SEATED INSIDE MY HEART
YOU WHO FILL EVERY CELL OF MY ENTIRE BEING
WITH YOUR PRESENCE LIGHT AND SONG
WHAT COULD SEPARATE WHAT I AM
FROM WHO THOU ART?

RID ME OF EGO
NOW AND FOREVER

THANK YOU FATHER

FOR WHEN I SAY 'I'
IT IS REALLY YOU
THAT I AM REFERRING TO
AS MY SELF

THANK YOU FATHER

O Heart of Hearts
when i look into their eyes
i see it is You alone
looking at your own Self
with exquisite joy and playfulness

for how long do You intend
to carry on this game?

DIVINE SAMURAI
HAVING REMOVED MY HEAD
YOU SKILLFULLY LEFT IT ON
SO AS NOT TO DRAW ATTENTION TO MY DEMISE
NOW I AM HERE ALONE INSIDE MY HEART
WITH YOU IN SECRET

HOW KIND IS YOUR SWORD

HOLY FATHER
YOU REPLACED MY SO-CALLED SANITY
WITH YOUR DIVINE MADNESS

PLEASE DO NOT RETURN IT
FOR THIS WOULD BE TRULY UNBEARABLE

BELOVED FATHER
I SURRENDER
THE DELUSION OF MYSELF
WITH ITS FALSE SENSE OF AUTONOMY
AND APARTNESS FROM YOU
THE ONE AND ONLY
TRUTH

O INEFFABLE ONE
RID ME OF THE ARROGANCE
AND PRIDE OF PERSONHOOD

EVEN THE VERY 'I AM'
IS OFFERED BACK TO YOU
THE SOURCE AND
WOMB OF ALL MANIFESTATION

ABSORB MYSELF IN YOU
FOR ALL ETERNITY

O FATHER
GRANT US THE RECOGNITION
THAT SICKNESS AND SUFFERING ARE
NOT MERELY OF THE FLESH
BUT OF THE MIND
AND THAT TRUE HEALING IS BESTOWED
BY LOOKING AGAIN
WITHOUT SHAME OR SEPARATION
INTO YOUR UNFATHOMABLE FACE

LET MY HEART BE PURE
AND FREE OF DOUBT

FINISH ME OFF FOR GOOD
FOR GOD

BELOVED FATHER
WHO DWELLS WITHIN THE SOUL
OF MY BEING
WHOSE NAME IS I AM
VENERATION TO YOUR HOLY NAME
THY KINGDOM IS HERE
THY WILL PREVAILS
THROUGHOUT THE EARTH
AS IT DOES IN THE HEAVENLY REALMS
OF MY SOUL

YOU OPEN YOUR HANDS
AND SATISFY THE HUNGER
OF ALL LIVING BEINGS
YOU HEAL ALL HEARTS OF SORROW
SO THEY IN TURN MAY SHOW FORGIVENESS
TO THOSE WHOSE MINDS
ARE SHROUDED IN IGNORANCE
OF THE TRUE SELF

BELOVED MOTHER
WHO IMPARTS TO ALL THE SENSE OF CHOICE
SO WE MAY FINALLY COME TO CHOOSE
YOU WHO ARE TRUTH
AND THUS FIND EVERLASTING
JOY AND FREEDOM

GLORY TO THY NAME
O TIMELESS TRUTH
FOR THINE IS THE KINGDOM
OF EXISTENCE
OF PEACE AND LOVE

ALL POWER AND GLORY
EMANATES FROM YOU ALONE
WHO IMPARTS TO ALL THE WISDOM
LIGHT LOVE AND COURAGE
TO PROCLAIM THEMSELVES
I AM

OM SHALOM
AMEN

O BELOVED
EVEN AS MY LIPS UTTER
THIS PRAYER TO BE MERGED IN YOU
I SEE THAT IT IS YOU ALONE
AS MY OWN SELF
IN WHOM ALL PRAYERS
AND THOSE OFFERING THEM
ARE PERCEIVED

WE ARE ALREADY TIMELESSLY ONE
THE INDIVISIBLE WHOLENESS

BLESSED IS MY SELF
O COMPASSIONATE FATHER

HEAVENLY FATHER WITHIN MY HEART
IN WHOM I APPEAR AS PRESENCE
AND APART FROM WHOM I HAVE NO REALITY
REMOVE ANY NOTION OF SEPARATENESS
SO THAT MY JOY IN YOU
REMAINS PURE
EVER COMPLETE AND
IRREVERSIBLE

BELOVED FATHER
YOU HAVE MADE FEAR MY ZEN STICK
SO THAT I REMAIN BLISSFULLY STATIONED
AT YOUR HOLY FEET

LIKE THIS MY MIND KNOWS
NO HOME APART FROM
THE DUST OF YOUR SOLES

THERE IS NO PLACE
THAT IS HIDDEN FROM YOU
O ALL SEEING ONE
LET WHATEVER APPEARS TO VEIL YOU
BE EXPOSED AS MERE ILLUSION

BY YOUR GRACE
I HAVE SEEN AND CONFIRMED THAT
THERE IS ONLY YOU

WHAT IS THERE LEFT
FOR ANY TO KNOW BUT THIS

BELOVED FATHER
WHY ALL THIS FUSS
THIS CONFUSION
WHEN THERE IS ONLY YOU?

MOTHER IS YOU
FATHER IS YOU
TIME IS YOU
CHANGE IS YOU
LIFE IS YOU
DEATH IS YOU
KNOWLEDGE IS YOU
IGNORANCE IS YOU
FRIEND IS YOU
ENEMY IS YOU
LIGHT AND DARKNESS IS YOU
WAKEFULNESS IS YOU
DREAM IS YOU
PAIN JOY AND WHATEVER ELSE IS LEFT
IS NOTHING BUT YOU

THE IMAGINABLE IS YOU
THE UNIMAGINABLE IS YOU
SENTIENT AND INSENTIENT
IS YOU ONLY

VERILY THE ONE
WHO COMPREHENDS ALL THIS
IS YOU
AND THE ONE WHO DOESN'T
IS NONE OTHER
THAN YOU

ALL THERE IS
ALL THAT EVER WAS
OR EVER WILL BE
IS YOU ONLY

THEY WHO ARE BIRTHED
AND TAKE THEIR BREATH IN YOU
ARE INSEPARABLY YOU

THE VERY CONSCIOUSNESS ITSELF
IN WHOM ALL THIS IS PERCEIVED
ARISES IN YOU ALONE

O UNFATHOMABLE ONE

O LORD
THIS IS YOUR DREAM
SO DO WHAT YOU WILL
HIDE ME INSIDE YOU
AND FORGET
WHAT YOU HAVE DONE

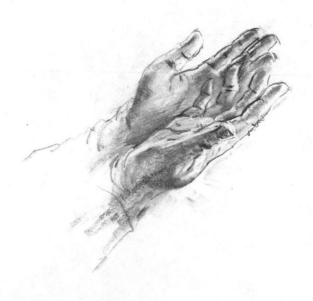

O LORD
LET ME NOT SEARCH FOR YOU
WITH EYES OF DISTANCE
WHEN YOU ALONE ARE
NEARER THAN INTIMACY
DISTANCELESS AND
ETERNAL

O Lord
FULLY FILL ME
LEAVE NO PLACE
FOR AN IDENTITY TO BE

EXCHANGE ME
FOR YOU

Beloved
you are both the
invitation and
my response to the
call home—

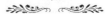

You pierced a hole
through the thick veil of delusion
and pulled me through into
your holy presence

Who is there left
to say these words
O Wordless One

O UNFATHOMABLE ONE
HAVING IMMERSED ME IN
YOUR DIVINE GRACE
ALL CONCEPTS GREAT AND SMALL
HAVE COLLAPSED LIKE
A HOUSE BUILT OF MATCHSTICKS
CAUGHT IN A STORM

HOW AMAZING THAT
ONE BREATH FROM MY LORD
IS ALL IT TOOK TO RAISE A MAN
FROM DEATH INTO
ETERNAL LIFE

Though I slept for countless time
in ignorance of my Lord
You kept an inner wakefulness hidden
as a seed inside my being

since You kissed this seed
into awakening
I am returned aware and
truly alive in You

I am today's Lazarus
but with this difference
this awakening is timeless
and imperishable

how unfathomable is
Your grace

O Unsparing and Merciful One

This is an emergency

Do not hesitate for a moment
to destroy all evil tendencies in my mind
Crush them mercilessly
so that I may breathe
completely in You
as You alone

amen

LET ME NOT PRAY
ON BEHALF OF THIS PERSON
SEEKING RELIEF HEALING
OR SALVATION

RATHER LET PRAYER BE OFFERED
IN CELEBRATION OF THE SEEING THAT
YOU ALONE EXIST

HOW MIRACULOUS!
ALTHOUGH THIS BODY APPEARS TO ACT
YOU HAVE IN FACT REMOVED ALL MY TASKS
AND ANOINTED MY BEING
WITH THE PEACE
AND PRESENCE OF
GOD

O HEAVENLY FATHER
ANY REMAINING SENSE OF A SOMEONE
TO WHOM THINGS HAPPEN
IS SURRENDERED
TO YOUR HOLY GRACE

EVEN IF EVERYTHING
IN THIS UNIVERSE
TURNS OUT TO BE FALSE
I KNOW I AM IN YOU AS ONE
AND NOTHING CAN REMOVE
THIS KNOWING

HOLY BELOVED
HAVING REVEALED WITHIN ME
THE IMPERMANENCE OF ALL THINGS
NOW ABSORB ME IN YOU
FOREVER

BELOVED FATHER
BEING EVER ONE WITH YOU
REMOVE ANY INSISTENCE IN ME
TO BE A PRIVATE OR SEPARATE ENTITY
FOR NOT ONE SINGLE MOMENT
IS WORTH LIVING
AS 'ME'

LET SUCH DELUSION BE LAID
AT YOUR FEET
O TIMELESS ONE

AT NIGHT I COLLAPSE IN BED
AND RISE NO MORE
TILL THE SUN COMES

LIKE THIS LET ME COLLAPSE
INSIDE YOUR HEART
AND RISE NO MORE AS MAN
BUT AS THE RISING SUN OF
THY GRACE

BELOVED FATHER
TO EVERYONE
YOU ARE COMPASSIONATE
THIS I HAVE SEEN WITH MY OWN EYES
EYES YOU MADE TO BEAR WITNESS
TO YOUR ETERNAL GREATNESS
AND LOVE

O Revealer of Truth
You showed me
the person is a figment of imagination
but the one who sees this
also cannot be found

Seeking self-realisation
it is found that
You are the very One
searching for yourself
through your own eyes
disguised as me

HOW MISCHIEVOUS!

MY FATHER
MY SELF
I LOVE YOU
I LOVE YOU
BUT LET THIS LOVE
BE WITHOUT SEPARATION
FOR THIS WOULD BE
UNENDURABLE

YOUR GRACE ALONE
CAN DISSOLVE MY DELUSIONS
SO ALL THAT REMAINS
IS PURE EMPTINESS
WHICH ALONE CAN RECEIVE AND REFLECT
YOUR BENEVOLENT LIGHT

LET YOUR HAND
BE MY HAND
LET YOUR LOVE
BE MY LOVE
LET MY BODY
BE YOUR BODY
LET MY MIND
BE YOUR MIND
LET MY HEART
BE YOUR HEART
LET MY VOICE
BE YOUR VOICE
LET MY SPIRIT
BE YOUR SPIRIT
LET MY LIFE
BE YOU
AMEN

O
WHITE FIRE
GRACE OF GOD
BURN THE RECOGNISED AND UNRECOGNISED
SEEDS OF DUALITY
MADE POISONOUS THROUGH EGO
BURN THE VERY ASHES OF EGO
LEAVING ONLY
THE IMMACULATE TRUTH
THOU ART

O
INDIVISIBLE ONE
NOTHING IS
BUT YOU

THOU ALONE ART

YOU ALONE
KNOW AND PROCLAIM
THIS

HEAVENLY FATHER

REPLACE THIS YOU WITH I
AND THIS I WITH
YOU

AMEN

O INSCRUTABLE ONE
YOU WASH MY MIND SO CLEAN
THERE IS NO MEMORY LEFT OF ME

TO MAKE MATTERS WORSE
YOU PERMIT ME TO CALL ME YOU

WHAT TROUBLE
YOU ARE CAUSING!

O HEART FATHER
AT TIMES THIS GREAT LOVE
YOUR HOLY PRESENCE
ROARS WITHIN MY HEART
LIKE ROLLING THUNDER
AND YET SUCH PEACE
PERMEATES MY BEING

WHO CAN FATHOM SUCH A THING?

HE ALONE WHO FEELS IT
KNOWS IT

FATHER WITHIN
FATHER WITHOUT
FATHER BEYOND
though i am ever one in You
i am also here in this world
with You through You
as your very presence
and in service to your will
in this mystical play called life
How inscrutable

HOLY LIGHT
YOU GUIDE ME
INTO YOUR PERFECTION
BY LIFTING MY MIND ABOVE
AND BEYOND THE PLAY OF OPPOSITES
INTO THE UNALTERABLE REALM
OF PURE BEING

WHO COULD DESERVE
SUCH GRACE?

YOUR KINDNESS
KNOWS NO BOUNDS

BELOVED
WHERE NEED I GO
WHAT NEED I SEEK
WHEN YOU ARE
MY ENTIRE AND COMPLETE
SATISFACTION

LOVING FATHER
GRANT THE WILL AND POWER HERE
TO CARE FOR THIS MORTAL TEMPLE
FOR THE SAKE OF SERVANTS
LOVERS AND SEEKERS OF THE
ONE GOD SELF

ENLIVEN THIS BODY
TO HOUSE HONOUR AND SERVE
THY INFINITE IMMORTAL
SPIRIT

O Compassionate Father
may they who are lost in the world
through ignorance of the Self
and thus suffer as ego
be now stirred into
awakening to the Real
through thy grace
and so be delivered
from the grip of darkness
Let them be timelessly renewed in You
O perfect Lord of the Universe

AMEN

O Lord Siva
LET ALL FACT-SEEMING DUALITY
BE BURNT FROM MY HEART SO THAT
ONLY THE Real REMAINS
UNTOUCHED AND IRREFUTABLE

DO THIS NOW
LEAVE NOTHING UNBURNT

As mere man
none is worthy
for vain is man and
blind to his true nature

You open the eyes of man
so he can see behind
the veil of self-delusion
and find You
the living Truth

O Dissolver of notions
empty us of ourselves
and leave us as
the nameless

Amen

O MY MIND
PUT YOUR TRUST IN GOD ALONE
WHO IS THE SELF OF ALL BEINGS
SHE IS THE SOURCE OF SENTIENCE
THE ONE WHO GIVES LIFE AND
JOY TO THE WORLD

O LORD
IT IS NOT MY IDEA
TO BE APART FROM YOU
AND YOU BEING INFINITE
IT CANNOT BE YOURS

WHOSOEVER IDEA IT IS
PLEASE DISREGARD AND
DISSOLVE ME IN YOU
FOREVER

O Sublime One
your grace has made it known here
I am not someone living life
I am life itself
and also the witness of life
and even beyond this
I Am

such exquisite understanding
you have revealed inside my heart
How auspicious!

HOLY ONE
YOU ARE THE LIVING GOD
WHO SHINES AS I
IN THIS FORM

LET ME SERVE YOU
THE ONE TRUE SELF

IT IS MY HIGHEST JOY
TO LIVE IN UNITY WITH YOU
AS TRUTH AND HARMONY
DANCING IN THIS WORLD
AS THE MIND HEART AND SPIRIT
OF THE UNIVERSE

HOLY MOTHER
HOLY FATHER
HOLY SPIRIT
SPARE ME THE ILLUSION
THAT EVEN ONE SECOND
BELONGS TO A ME
ALL IS YOU

I AM YOURS
I AM YOU

RID MY MIND OF
THE HABIT OF PROJECTION
AND INTERPRETATION

MAKE IT SILENT AND EMPTY
LIKE THE VAST BEING
OF GOD

O LORD
END THE IGNORANCE PRIDE AND
ARROGANCE OF BEING ME

LET MY KNOWING OF YOU
BE NOT OF THE MIND
BUT BE FULLY ALIVE
IN THE TIMELESS HEART
THAT IS THE TRUE
SELF

I AM SEEING THAT
ALL THIS IMPERSONAL MOVEMENT
IS BEING INTERPRETED
THROUGH THE MIND AS PERSONAL
DUE TO THE SENSE OF SEPARATION FROM YOU

DISPEL THIS DELUSION
MY LORD

DIVINE FATHER
HAVING BESTOWED UPON ME
THE CHRIST FAITH IN YOU
LET ME SHARE THIS DIVINE JOY
WITH ALL THOSE
WHO HUNGER TO MEET YOU
INSIDE THEIR HEARTS

EVEN TO SAY THANK YOU
THERE COMES A DULLNESS
FOR WORDS ARE WEAK

THEY COME AFTER THE FACT THAT
YOU MY OWN HEART ARE THE EXISTENCE
THE TIMELESS AND IMAGELESS
WITNESS OF ALL

O
LIGHT OF MY HEART
THROUGH YOUR GUIDING GRACE
I HAVE COME TO SEE THE WAYS OF MIND
THUS YOU RID MY HEART
OF THE LONGING FOR SATISFACTION
IN THE FIELD OF IMPERMANENCE

MY FULLNESS AND EMPTINESS
MY COMPLETE AND BLISSFUL
CONTENTMENT
YOU ARE

THERE IS NO LIFE
APART FROM
You

Loving and merciful Father
your compassion knows no bounds
May all who seek You
whatever paths they take
find and enter
your gracious
Heart

O Light of Life
show the way
beyond the person
into the true heart of God

Reveal the open door
so that all can pass through
into the imageless Self

BELOVED
WHAT A POWERFUL PLAY
YOU HAVE MADE
WHAT A MAGNIFICENT MIRACLE
YOU HAVE PERFORMED
TO HAVE SO FILLED MY HEART
WITH LOVE AND REVERENCE
FOR YOU

PLEASE LET ME
NEVER GO TO SLEEP

O JAH
LET ME NOT BE ATTACHED
TO ANY DESIRE
TO PRESERVE OR PERPETUATE
A LIFE OF DELUSION

LET ME REMAIN
IN THE BRIGHT LIGHT
OF YOUR SUPREME BEING
FOREVER MORE

SELAH

O
KING OF HEAVEN AND EARTH
RID ME OF THE HYPNOTIC INFLUENCE
OF THE PSYCHOLOGICAL MIND
ANNIHILATE ALL PRETENCE

LET HERE PREVAIL ONLY
THE CHRIST LIGHT
YOUR SIVA BEING

OM

BELOVED
I AM STILL BASKING
IN THE JOY OF YOUR FIRST KISS
STILL LIVING IN THE BREATH
OF MY FIRST GLIMPSE
OF YOU

O FORMLESS ONE

O
WOMB OF EXISTENCE
KEEP THIS LIFE
INSIDE YOU

HIDE ME
IN YOUR HEART

MERGE ME
IN YOUR BEING

DISPEL THE DELUSION
THAT ANYTHING BELONGS TO ME

WHO ELSE IS THERE BUT
YOU

FATHER
YOU OPENED THE DOOR—I AM
AND FOR A WHILE THE SENSE OF
GOING IN AND COMING OUT
COULD BE TASTED

NOW
YOUR GRACE IGNITES
THE RECOGNITION THAT I AM
IS INSEPARABLE FROM YOU

O
GUIDING LIGHT
YOU ARE THE WAY
INTO MY SELF
AND MY VERY SELF ITSELF

LET ME BE EFFORTLESSLY CONSCIOUS
IN THE BLISS OF
MY NON-DUAL BEING

FULLY REPLACE ME
WITH YOU ALONE
SO THAT MY LIFE IS YOU
SHINING THROUGH THIS FORM

YOU ARE THE LIGHT
INSIDE MY VERY LOOKING
THE KNOWER INSIDE MY KNOWING
THE VERY BREATH OF
MY BEING

REPLACE ME
LIKE THIS

BELOVED FATHER
YOU ALONE
ARE

THIS ALONE
IS TO BE RECOGNISED
IN THIS BODY
FOR WHICH PURPOSE
IT WAS MADE

THANK YOU
FOR THE LOVE THE GRACE
AND THE POWER OF SELF-INQUIRY
THAT YOU HAVE REVEALED
WITHIN ME

MAY IT SPEAK DIRECTLY
INTO THE HEARTS OF ALL
AND SHINE THE SEARING LIGHT OF CLARITY
THAT SO INSPIRES AND COMPELS ONE
TO FULL AWAKENING
IN YOU

GIVE US THE STRENGTH
TO BURN THE WEEDS OF ARROGANCE
THAT SPROUT SO QUICKLY ON THIS PATH
BURN AWAY ALL DISTRACTIONS
ALL EGOIC TENDENCIES

GIVE STRENGTH AND CLARITY
TO THOSE WHO SEEK YOU
LET THE HOLY SEEDS
YOU HAVE PLANTED HERE
GROW TO MIGHTY TREES
THAT CONTINUE TO SHARE THIS LOVE
TO SHINE BY YOUR LIGHT
IN THIS WORLD
AND BEYOND

I LEAVE THIS AT YOUR FEET
ONLY BECAUSE YOU ALONE
GRANT THE POWER THE COURAGE
AND THE FEARLESSNESS TO ASK THESE THINGS
IN THE NAME OF THE LORD JESUS CHRIST
AND ALL YOUR HOLY PROPHETS
SAINTS AND SAGES
YOU HAVE SENT TO THIS WORLD

AMEN

O ALL PERVADING ONE
REMOVE ALL IGNORANCE
AND VANITY HERE

TANALISE MY BEING
WITH YOU

DIVINE MOTHER
LIKE THE HEAVENS AT NIGHT
SILENT AND VAST
MERGE MY BEING
IN YOUR TIMELESS
IMMENSITY

ANOINT MY HEAD
WITH THE OIL OF YOUR HOLY SPIRIT
SO THAT I WILL NOT IMAGINE
EVEN FOR ONE MOMENT
THAT SEPARATION FROM YOU IS POSSIBLE

SEAL MY UNITY WITH YOU
FOR ALL TIME
AND BEYOND

AMEN

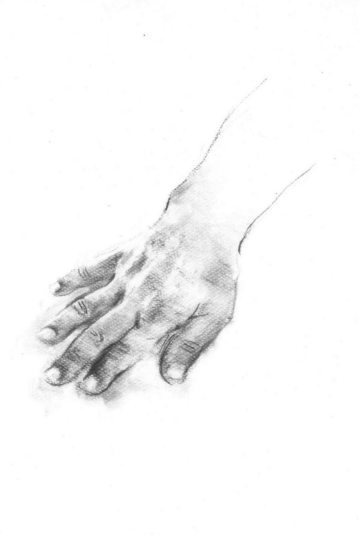

FATHER
YOU ALONE HAVE THE EYES
TO SEARCH MY HEART

TODAY REMOVE
WHATEVER REMAINS OF ME
LEAVE ONLY
YOU

OM

BELOVED
I AM NOTHING
WITHOUT
YOU

I AM NOTHING
WITH YOU

I AM NOTHING
ABSOLUTELY

Beloved
let me never imagine
i am something
let me never forget
i am nothing

What grace you have showered
upon my being
to have so filled this space
with You alone

BELOVED
WHILE THE WHOLE WORLD SLEEPS
I REMAIN AWAKE
IN AWE TO YOUR MAGNIFICENCE
THOUGH NONE CAN ATTAIN TO YOU
NONE EXIST APART FROM YOU

NONE BUT YOU ALONE
COULD REVEAL SUCH A WONDER
INSIDE MY HEART

BELOVED
YOU HAVE MADE MY HEART
THAT OF BOTH A DEVOTEE AND A JNANI
YOU ALONE KNOW HOW
YOU DID THAT

THANK YOU FATHER
FOR THE EXPERIENCE OF LIFE
FOR THE JOY AND
HARMONY OF BEING

THANK YOU
FOR YOUR EVER FLOWING GRACE
AND THIS DEEP CONTENTMENT
INSIDE MY HEART

AND BEYOND ALL THIS
THANK YOU FOR
THE SEAMLESS UNITY WITH YOU
AS UNBORN AWARENESS

You made
my heart and being
silent and happy
resting effortlessly
in your lap of
unfading grace

BELOVED FATHER
I EXIST ONLY BECAUSE OF YOU
I LIVE ONLY FOR YOU
THROUGH YOU
AS YOU

I IN I
FOREVER
YOU

HOLY MOTHER
YOU ARE THE SINGLE FORCE
INSIDE OUR HEARTS
NO POWER ON EARTH CAN
STAND AGAINST
YOU

HOW BLESSED WE ARE
YOU CAUSED YOUR LIGHT
TO SHINE UPON US
THAT WE COULD KNOW YOUR NAME
FEEL YOUR HOLY SPIRIT
SPEAK YOUR LANGUAGE
SEE WITH YOUR EYES
AND FEEL YOU
INSIDE OUR HEARTS

HOW BLESSED WE ARE
THAT WE ARE NOTHING
BUT YOU

ALLELUIA

HOLY FATHER
LET YOUR NAME
BE HOLY HERE ALWAYS

LET US WALK
IN THE LIGHT OF YOUR PREȘENCE
AND BRING HONOUR AND GLORY
TO YOUR NAME

LET EVERY STEP
EVERY BREATH
BE CONSCIOUSLY TAKEN
IN YOU

LET EVERY HEART
BE FULL OF GRATITUDE
FOR THE JOY
THE PRIVILEGE
AND THE EXPERIENCE
OF SERVING YOU

WHAT A GRAND ILLUSION
WHEN YOU ALONE
EXIST

ALHAMDULILLAH

THE LAST PRAYER

I AM FULL TO THE BRIM
BURSTING WITH LOVE
WITH GRATITUDE
WITH PEACE

I CANNOT CONTAIN ANYTHING
FOR YOU HAVE MADE ME EMPTY
AND YET SO FULL

EVERYTHING IN THIS WORLD
WILL PASS AWAY
EVERYTHING
IN THIS WORLD
WEARS AWAY
THINS AWAY
DISAPPEARS
BUT YOU

KEEP US MERGED IN YOU
LET IT BE SO FOR ALL TIME
AND BEYOND

May our lips never tire
of praising You

our hearts never tire
of loving You

our minds never tire
of thinking of You

May our feet never tire
of walking in You

May our being never tire
of resting in You
sleeping in You
rising in You

O Holy Spirit

Amen
Amen
Amen

BLESSINGS

WE GATHER TOGETHER HERE
IN THE CIRCLE OF LOVE AND TRUTH
IN THE NAME OF THE LORD
THE SUPREME BEING

WE GATHER IN A BOND OF LOVE
A BOND OF FAITH AND PURITY
A BOND OF COMPLETE TRUST
SURRENDER AND DEVOTION

WE PRAY THAT OUR PATH
CONTINUES TO BE THE PATH OF LIGHT
THAT EACH BREATH AND STEP BE TAKEN
IN FULL FAITH AND TRUST
IN THE LIGHT OF LOVE AND
THE POWER OF TRUTH

WE RISE ABOVE
THE LURE OF THE SERPENT'S VOICE
AND SO BECOME FREE
OF DELUSION AND DECEIT

WE PRAY THAT OUR HEARTS
REMAIN ABSORBED AND ONE WITH
THE SPIRIT OF GOD

LET OUR REALISATION
BE COMPLETE

O LORD
WE ABANDON OURSELVES
HERE AND NOW
FOREVER
AT THY HOLY FEET

AMEN

MAY ALL BE ETERNALLY ABSORBED
IN THE HOLY SPIRIT
I SAY—MAY ALL BE ETERNALLY ABSORBED
IN THE HOLY SPIRIT
SO BE IT

WHERE THERE REMAINS
A SENSE OF YOU AND I
MAY THAT BE ETERNALLY ABSORBED
IN THE HOLY SPIRIT
SO BE IT

WHEREVER THERE APPEARS TO BE
PERSONAL IDENTITY
LET THAT BE ETERNALLY ABSORBED
IN THE HOLY SPIRIT
SO BE IT

WHERE THERE MAY ARISE
THOUGHTS OF SEPARATION FROM THE ONE
LET THAT BE ETERNALLY ABSORBED
IN THE HOLY SPIRIT

MAY THESE BODIES THESE FORMS
BE ONLY VESSELS FOR THE HOLY SPIRIT
THE SPIRIT OF TRUTH

MAY ALL INTERACTIONS
AND EVERY ENCOUNTER
BE ONLY IN VENERATION OF
THE HOLY SPIRIT

WHERE THERE REMAINS
THE BELIEF IN DIVERSE CONCEPTS
ROOTED IN THE SENSE OF I AND OTHER
MAY THAT BE ABSORBED
IN THE HOLY SPIRIT
THE INFINITE ONE

WHERE THERE MAY STILL ARISE
ATTACHMENTS FOR WHAT IS PAST
WHAT WE ASPIRE FOR IN THE FUTURE
WHAT WE BELIEVE WE ARE NOW
MAY THAT BE ABSORBED
IN THE HOLY SPIRIT
IN THE DIVINE PRESENCE
IN THE INFINITE ONE

MAY MERE BELIEF BE REPLACED
BY DIRECT EXPERIENCE

MAY THE HUNGER FOR
TRUTH AND RIGHTEOUSNESS
BE SATISFIED

MAY THE DESIRE FOR LIBERATION
BE FULFILLED

SO BE IT

OM

SHANTI SHANTI SHANTI

3

LET OUR LIVES BE
TIMELESS GRATITUDE AND MIGHTY JOY

LET OUR HEART BE
GREAT PEACE AND HOLY SPIRIT

LET OUR NAME BE
AMEN

4

You are
the invisible and
indivisible
One

know this
with full certainty

there is no original doubt

You are the Truth
embodied

5

BE ANOINTED
WITH THE PRESENCE
OF THE HOLY SPIRIT

BE FILLED
WITH HIS LIGHT AND GRACE
THAT HIS PRESENCE OUTSHINE THE EGO
AND BRING YOUR SOUL TO
COMPLETE REST

MAY YOUR PATH BE STRAIGHT
MAY YOUR MIND BE FILLED WITH
WISDOM AND PEACE
AND YOUR HEART OVERFLOWING
WITH GRACE

BY THE POWER
OF YOUR FAITH AND TRUST
BECOME THE ANOINTED OF GOD
BE THE EMBODIMENT OF
HIS GRACE

WHEREVER YOU MAY FIND YOURSELF
BE THE HEART OF THAT PLACE

SO BE IT

OM

AMEN

6
HEALING

HOLY SPIRIT
LIVING HEALER
POWERFUL REDEEMER
GREAT SELF
SOUL OF SOULS
LIGHT OF ALL WORLDS
HEALING POWER OF THE UNIVERSE
FATHER OF THE LIVING CHRIST
SOURCE AND PRESENCE OF
THE HOLY ASSEMBLAGE OF SAGES
WOMB OF THE MANIFEST
CLEANSING LIGHT
LUMINOUS BEING
SACRED FIRE

WHEREVER THY
HEALING GRACE IS NEEDED
WHENEVER THY ATTENTION SOUGHT
LET THY CHILDREN BE REPLENISHED
BY THY REDEEMING TOUCH

BY THE LIGHT AND POWER
OF THE LIVING GOD
MAY THEIR HEARTS BE ABSORBED
IN THY PRESENCE
FOREVER MORE

O HEAVENLY ONE
YOU ALONE KNOW
THE NEED OF EACH SOUL

HARMONISE THEIR BEING IN YOU
SHELTER THEM
UNDER YOUR WINGS
COVER THEM
IN YOUR LOVING LIGHT
POWER AND GRACE

LET THEM BE FULLY
REPLENISHED
IN YOU

PROSTRATIONS
TO THE HOLY NAMES OF
THE SUPREME LORD OF THE UNIVERSE
THE IMMUTABLE SPIRIT OF TRUTH

AMEN

MAY YOUR LIFE
CONTINUE TO SHINE IN SWEET BLESSEDNESS
IN THE DEPTH OF THE SPIRIT
IN WISDOM AND PURE LOVE AND LIGHT

MAY YOU COME HOME TOTALLY
TO YOUR HEART'S KINGDOM
AND CONTINUE TO BE A LIGHT IN THIS WORLD

KNOW THAT THOSE WHO PUT
THEIR FULL TRUST IN GOD
THOUGH THEY SEEM TO WALK ON EARTH
ARE EVER ESTABLISHED IN
THE KINGDOM OF THE ALMIGHTY

8

O HEAVENLY ONE
I PLACE FULL TRUST AND FAITH
IN YOU ALONE

IT IS YOUR GRACE
THAT CONTINUES TO BLOSSOM
AS BEAUTY AND STRENGTH
INSIDE OUR HEARTS

IT IS BY YOUR GRACE ALONE
THAT OUR HEARTS ARE NOT COLOURED
BY DOUBT AND RESISTANCE
OR BY JUDGEMENT AND FEAR

YOU BROUGHT US TOGETHER
AS ONE FAMILY
SO THAT WE GROW IN YOU
IN THE WISDOM LIGHT AND POWER
OF THE LIVING SPIRIT
AND LOVE AND SUPPORT EACH OTHER
IN SPITE OF THE CHALLENGES
THAT COME IN LIFE

MAY THE FULL POWER OF THE HOLY SPIRIT
CONTINUE TO BE REVEALED
IN THE LIVES OF THE SANGHA
SO THAT EACH ONE SHINES UNIQUELY
IN THE LIGHT OF THE SUPREME

WE PLACE OUR HEARTS
INTO THE VERY HEART OF THE SELF
WE LIVE IN THE PRESENCE
AND EYES OF GOD
THE EYES OF TRUTH

O FATHER
YOU ARE MY STRENGTH
YOU ARE MY LIFE
YOU ARE THE VERY I INSIDE I AM
THANK YOU THAT YOU HEAR ME
AND THAT YOU CONTINUE
TO GUIDE THIS FAMILY
IN YOUR LIGHT

MAY YOUR GRACE AND PRESENCE
BE FELT EVER MORE STRONGLY
SO ALL MAY KNOW IRREFUTABLY
THAT YOU ALONE ARE
AND THUS BE FREE FROM
THE BITE OF SEPARATION

AS FROM THIS MOMENT
LET US REMAIN TIMELESSLY
IN YOU AS ONE

AMEN

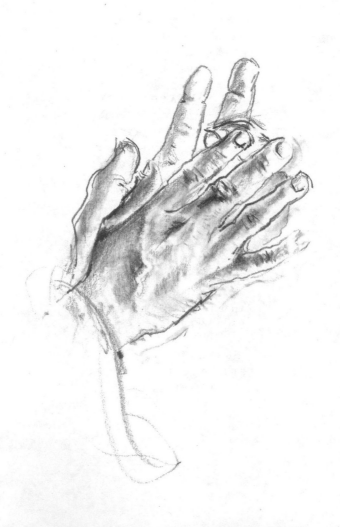

9

Om Namah Shivaya
OM
Om Sri Arunachala Siva
OM
Om Namo Bhagavate Sri Ramanaya
OM
Om Namo Bhagavate Sri Poonjaji
OM
Om Namo Bhagavate Sri Buddha
OM
Om Namo Bhagavate Sri Christ
OM
Om Namo Bhagavate Sri Krishna
OM
Om Namo Bhagavate Sri Anandamayi Ma
OM
Om Namo Bhagavate Sri Yogi Ramsuratkumar
OM
Om Namo Bhagavate Sri Ma Devaki
OM
Om Namo Bhagavate Sri Nisargadatta Maharaj
OM
Om Namo Bhagavate Sri Bankei
OM
Om Namo Bhagavate Sri Ram
OM
Om Shanti Shanti Shanti Om

MY BLESSING IS THAT ALL
WHO COME IN SEARCH OF TRUTH
WHOSE MINDS AND HEARTS BEAT FOR
THIS MOST IMPORTANT DISCOVERY
COME SWIFTLY TO
THE FULL REALISATION OF THE TRUTH
INSIDE THEIR HEARTS

MAY YOUR LIGHT SHINE BRIGHTLY
MAY YOU BE TIMELESSLY HAPPY
AND YOUR PEACE BE UNDISTURBED

MAY YOU GROW IN WISDOM
LOVING KINDNESS AND COMPASSION
AND MAY ALL WHO MEET YOU ON THE WAY
BE PROFOUNDLY TOUCHED AND INSPIRED
BY YOUR OPENNESS
YOUR LOVE AND SILENCE

MAY YOUR HEART BE
A LIGHT IN THIS WORLD
FOR BLESSED IS THE ONE WHOSE LIFE
IS THE EVIDENCE OF TRUTH

SO AS YOU GO YOUR WAY
MAY YOU COME TO SEE THAT
THERE IS NO END TO AUSPICIOUSNESS
THAT THIS FLOWER OF GRACE
CONTINUES OPENING
AND THAT YOU WILL NEVER FAIL
NOR FALL FROM HIS GRACIOUS PRESENCE

THIS IS MY HEART'S BLESSING TO YOU

IF YOU HAVE CHOSEN WHAT IS TRUE
I STAND BY YOU
TRUST THAT
BE ONE WITH THAT

MAY GRACE ALWAYS BE WITH YOU

MAY THE FACE OF GOD
ALWAYS SHINE UPON YOU
AND FILL YOU WITH
PEACE

SO BE IT

MAY ALL BEINGS
AWAKEN SWIFTLY TO THE SINGLE TRUTH
FROM WHICH ALL EMANATES

MAY ALL BE HAPPY
IN THE KNOWING THAT
WE ARE ONE FAMILY OF BEING
WITH ONE COMMON HEART
A HEART OF IMAGELESS PERFECTION
BEATING INSIDE THE
INFINITE

ACCORDING TO YOUR HEART'S PLEA
YOUR HEART'S LONGING
IN THE PRESENCE OF
THE SUPREME LORD OF THE UNIVERSE
THE HOLY SPIRIT
THE SPIRIT OF TRUTH
THE PRESENCE OF THE LORD JESUS CHRIST
AND ALL THE SAGES
SAINTS AND PROPHETS WHO HAVE COME
INTO THE HUMAN KINGDOM
I BAPTISE YOU IN THE NAME OF
TRUTH AND RIGHTEOUSNESS

MAY YOUR MIND BE PURE
AND YOUR HEART ALWAYS LIVE
IN THE JOYOUS GLORY OF GOD

MAY ALL THE FORCES
THAT COULD BE AN OBSTACLE
BE SWEPT ASIDE BECAUSE
THE LIGHT THAT EMANATES FROM YOU
THE LIGHT THAT YOU ARE
DISPELS ALL IGNORANCE AND DARKNESS

WHEREVER YOU GO
MAY YOUR HEART AND BEING
BE IMBUED WITH
THE PRESENCE OF THE LORD

MAY YOUR STEPS BE SURE
AND WHATEVER THE CIRCUMSTANCES
OBSERVE THAT ALL UNFOLDS
IN THE PRESENCE OF
THE UNCHANGING GROUND OF BEING

MAY YOU ALWAYS BE ESTABLISHED
IN UNITY WITH THE SUPREME
MAY YOU RISE IN THE JOY
OF THAT DISCOVERY

MAY YOUR SPIRIT
BLOSSOM BLOOM AND BEAR FRUIT
IN THE FORMLESS EDEN OF
THE LIVING GOD

SO BE IT

OM NAMAH SHIVAYA

MAY YOU DISCOVER THE LIFE
WHICH IS FREE OF SORROW

MAY YOUR MIND BE ILLUMINED
IN THE TRUTH

MAY YOU CONQUER THE FEAR OF DEATH

MAY YOU NEVER BE ASHAMED
OF THE PRESENCE OF THE HOLY SPIRIT
NOR FEEL THE NEED TO DEFEND YOURSELF
IN ANY PERSONAL WAY

MAY YOUR TRUST BE GREAT
YOUR HEART FULL OF LOVE
AND MAY YOU CARRY THE PERFUME
OF THE LORD'S PRESENCE
WHEREVER YOU GO

THIS IS THE PRAYER
THAT I MAKE FOR YOU
IN THE NAME OF
THE HOLY SPIRIT OF GOD

SO BE IT

OM

SHANTI SHANTI SHANTI

To love God
with all one's mind
and all one's heart
so there remains
nothing but radiant presence
emanating from Him
—unborn Awareness

to be so absorbed in Him
to die in Him while alive
is to be resurrected
in the immaculate presence
and glory of the living God

May our destiny be so

amen

How blessed we are
that we are nothing
but you

Beloved —
May you grow in wisdom
Loving Kindness & Compassion
and may all who meet you on the way
Be profoundly touched & Inspired
by your Openness
Your Love & Silence
Your grace and
Wisdom and Love
— Amen —

O Lord of Hearts
thank you
for allowing me
to be Nothing

Beloved

Let me exist by
the light of your
Eyes Only —

You are the
invisible & indivisible One
Know this with
full Certainty
There is no original doubt
You are the truth
Embodied

Allelujah

Amen

Advaita Zen master **Mooji** was born in Jamaica in 1954. As a teenager, he moved to London, UK, where he worked as a street portrait artist and then as an art teacher. After an encounter with a Christian mystic inspired him to "walk out of his life," Mooji traveled to India, where he met his master Sri H. W. L. Poonja, or Papaji, a direct disciple of the great Advaita master Ramana Maharshi. At Papaji's feet, whatever remained of an active ego within Mooji was finally uprooted.

Mooji is unlike anyone else you are likely to meet, for his presence exudes a loving compassion and devotion, and compels one to question one's very nature and existence. People from all walks of life are deeply touched by this indefinable presence. Each one who meets Mooji with a genuine urge for pure understanding and freedom is pulled by the profundity of his unconditional love and the power of his pointings into the recognition of the infinite Self we already are.

THE MALA OF GOD

Original English version first published in July 2015 by

Mooji Media Publications

A trade name of Mooji Media Ltd., UK

Distributed in Canada by Raincoast Books

Copyright © 2017 by Mooji Media Ltd., UK
           Non-Duality Press
           An imprint of New Harbinger Publications, Inc.
           5674 Shattuck Avenue
           Oakland, CA 94609
           www.newharbinger.com

Edited by Sivaganga, Rose, Sumantra, Gayatri, Zenji, Parvati, Samadhi and Krishnabai
Drawings by Mooji Baba
Design and layout by Sivaganga, Rose, Leonardo
Photographs by Leonardo, Illah, Yamuna
Design support by Jyoti, Bhagavati, Nitya

Printed in Canada

British Library Cataloguing in Publication Data.
A catalogue record for this book is available from the British Library.

18   17   16

10   9   8   7   6   5   4   3   2   1

MORE BOOKS for the SPIRITUAL SEEKER

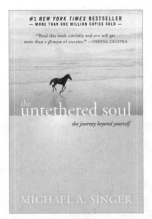
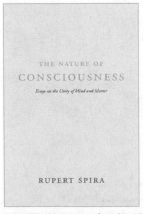
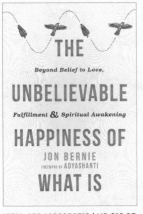